SERIES 205

In this book, we will look at hedgerow picnics,
unexpected houseguests and hibernating
hedgehogs, as we explore the
beauty of the autumn.

LADYBIRD BOOKS

UK | USA | Canada | Ireland | Australia
India | New Zealand | South Africa

Ladybird Books is part of the Penguin Random House group of companies
whose addresses can be found at global.penguinrandomhouse.com.

www.penguin.co.uk   www.puffin.co.uk   www.ladybird.co.uk

 Penguin
Random House
UK

First published 2020

002

Copyright © Ladybird Books Ltd, 2020

Printed in Italy

A CIP catalogue record for this book is available from the British Library

ISBN: 978–0–241–41616–7

All correspondence to:

Ladybird Books
Penguin Random House Children's
One Embassy Gardens, 8 Viaduct Gardens
London SW11 7BW

MIX
Paper from
responsible sources
FSC® C018179
www.fsc.org

What to Look For in
Autumn

A Ladybird Book

Written by Elizabeth Jenner

Illustrated by Natasha Durley

Birds on the Broads

It is the beginning of autumn, and it is getting busy on the Norfolk Broads! As summer turns to autumn, the bird population swells. The winter migrant birds, such as the Bewick's swan, have arrived to claim the wetlands for the autumn and winter. At the same time, summer migrant birds, such as the common tern, are preparing to leave, and will soon fly away to warmer countries in big, swooping flocks.

These Bewick's swans have come from Siberia, where they breed during the summertime, and will stay in the United Kingdom for the winter. When the weather in Siberia turns cold, the swans migrate to these milder wetlands, bringing their young with them.

The young swans, or cygnets, have grey feathers and pink bills. When they are fully grown, their feathers will turn white and their bills will become yellow and black. The pattern on the bill of a Bewick's swan is like a fingerprint – no two birds have the same one.

The swans will roost on the wetlands every night. However, during the autumn days, they often head to nearby fields in search of leftover crops to eat, such as potatoes and grain.

Back to school

After the long summer holidays, it is time to go back to school. Uniforms are laid out, book bags are packed and children all over the country get ready for the first day of the school year.

As children travel to school, the leaves on the trees above them transform from green to red with each passing day. The trees have sensed the seasons changing, and are preparing for the winter.

The green colour of leaves is produced by a chemical called "chlorophyll". This helps trees to create food and energy from sunlight, through a process called "photosynthesis". In the autumn, when the days become colder, shorter and darker, some trees stop producing chlorophyll as a way to save energy. Because of this, the other chemicals in the leaves, such as yellow and orange carotenes, become more obvious and the leaves change colour.

The bright orange and red leaves will gradually dry up and drop off later in the autumn. Trees that go through this cycle are known as "deciduous" trees. By contrast, some trees keep their green leaves all year round, and are known as "evergreen" trees.

Ploughing the fields

In the countryside, this blanket of green fields is becoming a patchwork of colour. It is time for the farmers to harvest their remaining crops and to plough the fields. One by one, wheat fields are harvested, and the wheat is taken away. Once the field is empty, ploughing can take place.

A plough is a machine that turns and loosens the soil. It brings fresh nutrients to the surface and buries any remains of the old crop and weeds, which will then rot and return leftover nutrients to the earth.

After the soil has been ploughed into fresh, rich furrows, the farmer will sow new wheat seeds, ready to sprout in the spring. It's important to plough soil before sowing new seeds, as this creates the best conditions for growing.

In the past, ploughs were drawn by horses or cattle, but today you are more likely to see them attached to a tractor. Ploughing is hard work, but some farmers make it fun by organizing ploughing matches. These matches see who can plough the best or fastest while using a variety of machines and techniques.

Harvesting the allotment

Gardeners everywhere are busy harvesting their crops. They pick the autumn fruit and vegetables in their gardens, and prepare their plots for the next growing year.

In gardens and allotments, apples and pears hang low on the branches of trees, ready to be collected. Potatoes and carrots are dug up from garden beds, and beetroots are pulled from the ground with a gentle twist. The last of the fresh lettuce leaves and runner beans must also be picked.

It is important to harvest crops, as this makes sure the food does not go to waste and helps the natural growing cycle of the plants. Once the vegetables in these beds have been picked, the allotment gardeners will break up the soil and remove any weeds, using a metal tool called a "hoe". They may also sow seeds for new plants, such as cabbages.

Plants use up a lot of the nutrients in the soil during spring and summer, so autumn is also a time to help the soil to recover. Gardeners may leave beds empty, or "fallow", so they are rested. Or they might sprinkle compost – a rich material made of decayed plants – on their plots to replenish the soil, ready for the next growing year.

1. "Rainbow" Swiss chard
2. "Autumn king" carrot
3. "Worcester Pearmain" apple
4. "Polestar" runner bean
5. "Conference" pear
6. Hand fork and trowel
7. "Carolina ruby" sweet potato
8. "Boltardy" beetroot

Mushroom season

The round, white objects in this field may look like strange stones, but they are actually giant puffball mushrooms. Mushrooms grow from organisms called "fungi". Since they like cool, damp conditions, there are lots dotted around the edges of fields and woodlands during the autumn months.

The giant puffball is one of the easiest mushrooms to spot, due to its bulbous shape and huge size. They often grow to 50 centimetres (1 ft, 8 in.) wide, and some giant puffballs have even been known to hit 150 centimetres (4 ft, 11 in.)! The younger mushrooms are firm and white inside, but as they get older, the inside starts to rot and turn into millions of tiny brown spores. These spores will eventually be released and will grow into new fungi.

Some of the Holstein-Friesian cows in this field are pregnant, and will soon give birth to their babies, known as "calves". The cows are part of a dairy herd of cattle, and they are kept for their milk supply. A cow only produces milk when she has a calf to feed, and the traditional calving season is spring. However, dairy farmers often have an autumn calving season as well, so that their herd will produce milk that can be sold all year round.

Feasting on the hedgerows

In September, hedgerows everywhere become bright and heavy with berries. It is picnic time for these lucky birds! The finches and tits love to eat the juicy blackberries, plump blue sloes and shiny clusters of elderberries, and they are even able to prise the fat cobnuts from their green husks. Walkers, ramblers and hikers may even stop to join the feast, picking a tempting blackberry as they pass by.

Plants often rely on birds to carry away their seeds and scatter them in new areas in order to grow. To attract as many birds as possible, some plants hide their seeds inside colourful berries to disguise them as delicious snacks. These seeds are indigestible, so when a bird has flown away to a new area, the seeds will reappear in their droppings and hopefully grow into new plants.

Hedgerows are made up of long rows of bushes. They are often used as boundary lines to divide fields or mark roads. Some are hundreds of years old, and they provide important shelter and food for a lot of wildlife, including small mammals, such as hedgehogs and voles, and many different birds and insects.

1. Elderberries
2. Cobnut
3. Willow tit
4. Sloe berries
5. Greenfinch
6. Chaffinch
7. Blackberries

Swallow migration

The swallows are getting restless. It is almost time for their annual winter migration. The falling temperatures and shorter days tell them to start gathering together to prepare for their trip. See how they flutter about overhead and sit waiting on telephone wires.

These swallows will be flying 5,000 miles (8,000 km) to South Africa for the winter. The journey will take them about six weeks. In huge flocks, they will fly during daylight hours, covering about 200 miles (320 km) a day, and will roost overnight in reed beds along the way.

This long journey can be dangerous. The flock can run into storms, and some birds will become too tired to fly and will collapse from exhaustion. Although swallows eat insects while they fly, they sometimes pass through areas like the Sahara Desert, where food is scarce. If a swallow hasn't built up enough fat reserves in its body to give it energy during the journey, it can starve.

However, every year many swallows arrive safely to a warm welcome in South Africa. There they will pass the winter months in the sunshine, feasting on insects, before returning to the United Kingdom in April.

Unexpected houseguests

As the weather grows colder, some uninvited visitors could appear in your home. A giant house spider might sneak up the wall, or you might notice ladybirds crawling along the windowsills. Crane flies might take advantage of an open door and fly inside, wings flapping and long legs dangling. All of these creatures are seeking a warm place to rest, and the corners and ceilings of our houses are tempting homes.

Harlequin ladybirds look for a place to hibernate over the winter. Originally from Asia, they are a recent arrival to the United Kingdom and, in just a few years, they have become the second most common ladybird species. The most common native ladybird is the seven-spot ladybird, which hibernates outside in trees or leaf litter, but the harlequin prefers to spend the winter inside buildings. Look for them clustered in corners of rooms and windows.

Due to its appearance, the crane fly is also called "daddy long-legs" in the United Kingdom. At this point in the year, crane flies have already mated and laid their eggs in the grass outside. They are now near the end of their lives. Crane flies are harmless – although, if one flies out when you're not expecting it, it can give you a surprise!

1. Seven-spot ladybird
2. European crane fly
3. Giant house spider
4. Harlequin ladybird

The bug hotel

Welcome to the bug hotel! This winter wildlife home has been made from wood, bricks, stones and leaves for insects, minibeasts and other small garden creatures.

In modern buildings and parks, there are not many places for minibeasts to hide during the winter. Neat gardens, smooth concrete walls and open spaces don't provide many cracks and crevices for insects to hide in. As the weather gets colder, minibeasts need safe, protected places to shelter, and bug hotels are often the answer.

Bug hotels attract lots of different creatures because they are made from many materials. Bricks and wooden pallets create sturdy layers. Dead wood and bark are perfect for spiders, woodlice and centipedes. Corrugated cardboard attracts lacewings, and dry leaves and straw will entice ladybirds. The small holes in bamboo tubes become homes for solitary bees, while larger holes made with stones and tiles provide cool, damp apartments for frogs and toads.

Once a hotel is tall enough, it's time to put on the roof. Old roof tiles or slates will protect the inhabitants from winter winds and rain. Once the roof is secured, simply watch and wait for the guests to arrive!

Woodland games

When walking through parks and woods in October, keep an eye out for shiny, red-brown conkers nestling in their prickly green cases. These are the seeds of the horse chestnut tree.

The tree drops conkers so that they will grow into new trees, but some will have a different destiny. The biggest and best conkers are collected by children in order to play a game.

The game "Conkers" has been played in the United Kingdom for at least 150 years. A child will drill a hole through a brown horse chestnut seed and thread it to a piece of string to create their conker. They then take turns striking other children's conkers until one of the conkers breaks. Some contestants prefer to soak their conkers in vinegar first, to make them harder and less likely to break – although this might be seen as cheating!

Conkers aren't the only tree seeds that are fun to play with at this time of year. Watch the seeds from the sycamore tree as they twirl down from the branches. The seeds sit between a pair of wings called "keys", which, when dropped, make the seeds spin like tiny helicopter blades. Pick them up and throw them high into the air to make them dance!

The battle of the red deer

Deep bellows echo over the Scottish Highlands, startling the mountain hares. In a herd of red deer, the largest stag is the dominant male, and he is looking to defend his position. He struts and roars, tossing his antlers from side to side, daring the young male bucks to try to fight him.

One brave buck takes on the challenge. The two deer clash, bowing their heads to lock antlers and then pushing each other back and forth. It looks and sounds like a violent fight, but it is really just a show of power. If the young buck wins, he will move up the pecking order in the herd, and he will have the right to mate with more female deer. This is known as "the rut", and it happens at this time every year.

The male deer grow their antlers every summer in preparation for this battle. Their antlers are made of a hard, honeycomb-like bone. Once the rut has taken place, the stags no longer need their antlers. These impressive decorations will start to become weak at the base and will eventually drop off. If you take a walk in a deer park after the autumnal rut, you might spot a fallen antler or two on the ground. The stags will start to grow new antlers again in the spring, which appear as soft, velvety nubs on their foreheads.

Pheasant season

A tractor trundles along the edges of these fields, cropping the branches of the hedges. The hedges have grown big and unruly during the summer, and they need a trim to be kept under control! This is the best time to trim them, because the bird-breeding season is over, and the bushes have finished their growth cycle for the year and have stopped producing leaves and fruit. Trimming them now will cause less stress and damage to the plants.

Down on the ground, a pheasant cock, with his colourful head, and a tawny pheasant hen make their escape from the moving tractor. Pheasants are a common sight in the British countryside at this time of year. The landowners of big estates often breed pheasants so they can later be hunted for sport. This is why they are known as "game" birds.

The pheasant season usually lasts from October to January or February. Pheasants are released into the wild at the start of the season by the gamekeeper, and they can then be hunted during the season at organized events called "shoots". After the shoots, the pheasants are often given to the hunters to take home.

In the pumpkin patch

In October, heavy, orange pumpkins squat in the fields beneath green leaves, waiting to be picked. A pumpkin is the fruit of a type of squash plant. Squash fruits come in all shapes, sizes and colours. They ripen in the autumn, and a lot of people bake them or turn them into tasty soups.

However, these pumpkins may well be used for something a little spookier! Halloween has been marked in the United Kingdom for centuries, and it falls on 31 October every year. It was originally an occasion to remember the dead, but now it is a celebration of all things scary.

Some children dress up in costumes and go from house to house, trick-or-treating. People might hold parties with games, such as apple bobbing, and others might carve pumpkins into grinning faces called "jack-o'-lanterns".

To make a jack-o'-lantern, scoop out the fleshy insides of the pumpkin, and then carve a face into the rind. Finally, place a candle inside and light it, so that the pumpkin's grin flickers and glows in the dark. Originally, these lanterns were made of other vegetables, like swedes and turnips, and then placed on windowsills to scare off evil spirits, but today pumpkins are used as festive Halloween decorations.

1. "Turban" squash
2. "Crown prince" squash
3. "Kabocha" squash
4. "Sweet lightning" squash
5. "Carnival" squash
6. "Connecticut field" pumpkin

Lighting up the skies

In early November, amid a cacophony of pops and bangs, a riot of colourful sparks fills the night sky. Bonfire Night happens on 5 November, which is when Guy Fawkes' unsuccessful plot to blow up the Houses of Parliament in 1605 is remembered in the United Kingdom. All over the country, people wrap up warm and gather outside to watch firework displays. A doll, or "guy", may be burned on a bonfire. Toffee apples are a popular snack, and children wave fizzling sparklers in the air to make patterns.

Above these dazzling celebrations, a round, yellow moon hangs low in the sky. It is a full moon, which means the whole of the moon is visible. Each month, the moon moves through a set of different phases, appearing to gradually increase in size and then decrease again, before disappearing entirely. In reality, though, the moon is always there, even when we can't see it.

The moon circles the earth and, as it travels, its distance from the sun changes. The sun's light falling on the moon affects how much of the moon's surface we are able to see. As the moon becomes bigger, moving from a crescent to a full moon, we say the moon is "waxing". As it becomes smaller again, shrinking to a sliver before vanishing into a new moon, we say it is "waning".

Autumn hoards

As the end of autumn draws near, animals start to prepare for the change of season. In winter, there is less food available, so many animals start to gather provisions now.

Grey squirrels go in search of acorns for their store. Squirrels are selective about the nuts that they pick. They smell the nuts to check if they are ripe and throw away any that feel too light. Lightness might mean that the nut has already been eaten by a smaller creature, such as an insect larva. Once it has found a good acorn, the squirrel will bury it in soft soil, patting down the earth around it.

Squirrels bury each acorn they find in a separate place. This means that if one stash is discovered, they still have other acorns to rely on. However, squirrels often have so many stores that they forget about some of them! Come spring, any leftover acorns will sprout into seedlings and perhaps grow into new oak trees.

1. Eastern grey squirrel
2. English oak leaf
3. Common ash leaf
4. Douglas fir leaf
5. Wood mouse
6. Common beech leaf
7. Acorn (nut of the English oak tree)
8. Horse chestnut leaf
9. Death cap mushroom

1

2

3

4

5

6

x

7

8

9

Hedgehogs in hibernation

In November, it is time for the hedgehogs to find cosy places to hibernate. They will find warm, safe places to make a nest, such as log piles, compost heaps or artificial hedgehog houses made by humans, and curl up for a long winter rest.

For hedgehogs, the process of hibernation is a way of making sure that they can survive the winter while food is scarce. During the autumn, a hedgehog will eat as much as possible, to build up the fat stores in its body. Then, once it is safely settled into its nest, the hedgehog will drop its body temperature to match its surroundings. All of its body functions, including its breathing and heartbeat, will slow down as well. This will enable the hedgehog to save a lot of energy so it can survive on its fat stores until spring.

If the weather becomes mild during the winter, hedgehogs may occasionally leave their nests to find a quick bite to eat. Otherwise, they will stay safely tucked up in their nests in hibernation for the entire season.

Plenty of other animals also prepare for hibernation at this time of year, including bats, dormice, bumblebee queens, ladybirds, frogs and grass snakes.

Starlings in flight

As it gets dark, a giant cloud of tiny, black flecks twists and turns in the late-autumn sky. As it swoops and swirls, the shape splits apart and winds back together again and again. This cloud is actually a flock of starlings, coming together in a dramatic display called a "murmuration".

Starlings stay together during the autumn and winter. They choose places to live where thousands of birds can roost together, in areas such as reed beds and woodlands. They gather to keep warm and exchange information about the best places to feed.

Every evening, before they roost for the night, starlings take to the sky for this breathtaking display. Nobody knows exactly why starlings do this. Some bird experts, known as "ornithologists", believe that the birds are signalling the route to a safe roost for other starlings. Others think it helps protect the starlings from predators, such as peregrine falcons, who will be confused by the display and unable to pick out a single bird to target. Either way, murmurations are a beautiful, natural mystery.

Despite these large crowds, there are far fewer starlings in the United Kingdom than there used to be. Many of their natural roosting and feeding sites have disappeared, due to an increase in built-up areas, and they are now endangered here.

New life on the coast

On this Norfolk beach, female grey seals have come to shore to give birth to their pups. The seals set up big groups, or "colonies", along the coastline, where the newborns can be raised in the safety of a group.

The colonies are noisy places. Pups cry loudly, demanding to be fed. Mother seals howl at each other, protecting their young. All the while, male seals, looking to mate, patrol the beach, making huffing noises like steam trains!

When the pups are born, they have fluffy white fur. This is because many years ago they would have been born in snowy conditions, and their fur would have helped to camouflage them from predators.

They are fed on milk from their mothers, who stay with them for their first month. After this, the mothers will leave the pups in the colony and go back to the sea to feed on fish and to mate again.

The young seals will stay on the shore for the next few weeks, until they have tripled in size and their grey adult coats have grown. Then, they will also take to the sea to learn to swim and fish for themselves.

The salmon run

Can you spot the flashes of silver in this cascading waterfall? At this time of year, Atlantic salmon can often be seen leaping out of the water in an attempt to scale waterfalls. Salmon can jump very high – up to four times their own length. The largest fish will easily make it to the top of the waterfall on their first attempt, but the smaller fish will crash back down to the bottom and be forced to try again and again until they manage it.

Every year, Atlantic salmon make this difficult journey upriver from the sea. They wait for the heavier autumn rainfalls to swell the rivers, so that swimming up the rocks and waterfalls will be as easy as possible. Then, they gather at the mouth of the river to begin their trek against the current.

These fish were born in this river, and have spent their adult lives out at sea, growing and maturing. Once they are ready to spawn and produce eggs of their own, they return to their own spawning grounds to do so.

Once the females have laid their eggs and the males have fertilized them, many of the salmon will die. Those that survive will have a much easier journey back out to sea, swimming with the river rather than against it.

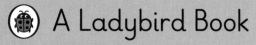

A Ladybird Book

collectable books for curious kids

What to Look For in Spring

9780241416181

What to Look For in Summer

9780241416204

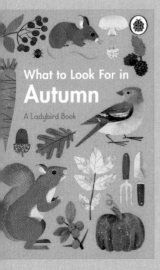

What to Look For in Autumn

9780241416167

What to Look For in Winter

9780241416228